THE
LUNAR
YEAR

MOON MAGIC
THROUGH THE
SEASONS

ALISON DAVIES

Illustrated by
Anastasia Stefurak

Hardie Grant

QUADRILLE

CONTENTS

Introduction 6

INTRODUCTION

We watch in wonder, gazing up at the pearlescent beauty of the Moon. We ponder its phases, the gentle grace with which it shifts shape before our eyes. We contemplate its power and let the soft glow inspire us. We tell tales and create myths to explain its value, we give it layers of meaning and attempt to capture its essence in artistic form. We have even landed upon it. The Moon's presence is ingrained within our psyche, because it has always been there. Since the dawn of the history of the Earth it has taken its place in the sky, helping to shape the world we now live in. From powerful lunar rhythms to the ebb and flow of the tides, the Moon's influence is more potent than most could imagine.

Moonlight, which is actually a reflection of the Sun's light and not something the Moon gives off naturally, may induce romantic notions, but it also has an extraordinary effect upon living organisms, encouraging procreation, and helping them to find their way. The African dung beetle is a prime example – it uses the polarized light of the Moon to navigate in a straight line, giving it the edge on predators, and helping it reach the safety of home quickly. The spectacular sight of corals spawning upon the Great Barrier Reef is something of a lunar event, too, as it always follows a full moon and can even be witnessed from space. The tides are one of the most common ways we can see the Moon's power at work. The gravitational pull of the Moon causes a bulge in the oceans on the nearest and furthest sides of the Earth, a catalyst for the tidal swing from high to low, and so we experience both in the course of a day.

The ancients embraced the magical might of the Moon, taking it to their hearts, and performing rites and rituals to harness the energy of each specific phase – practices that still hold sway today. Even scientists agree that the lunar cycle causes erratic sleep patterns and mood swings, which have the capacity to shape our daily experiences. With this in mind, it makes sense that we can connect with the power of the Moon and work with its phases. We can tap into the flow of energy and create habits and rituals that will not only affect our wellbeing, but also help us in other areas. From triggering the imagination and harnessing our innate creativity, to unleashing our intuition and helping us feel more confident, wherever we are in the cycle of life.

This book charts the path of the Moon through the sky, and through each season. It provides monthly highlights and lunar aspects on which you can focus and use to enhance each day. It delves into moon myths and magic from around the world and offers a mystical glimpse of the many facets of this lunar orb. From monthly spells to new and full moon rituals, you also will learn about the gods and goddesses associated with the Moon, and the folklore and superstitions that have made it such an integral part of human existence. You'll also find a 6-Year Moon Cycle Calendar (see page 140), which charts each of the main phases, every month for the next six years, so that you can work out the best days to work with the Moon, depending on what you'd like to achieve.

continued . . . . .

The lunar impact upon the planet is clear to see, but what is even more wondrous is the effect the Moon can have on you. It doesn't matter who you are or what your situation may be, when you open your heart and mind to the Moon, you invite enchantment into your life. You bathe in the radiance of its glow and allow yourself to shine. So step into the light, embrace the luminescence and navigate your own path through the lunar year.

THE MOON CYCLE

The Moon reflects light. Depending on where it is in its cycle of movement around the Earth, a different portion of its surface is illuminated by the Sun at any one time. As it moves, we see different aspects of it, depending on which side the sunlight hits. When the light reflects from the far side of the Moon's surface, we don't see anything – this is a 'new moon'. When it hits the near side, we experience a 'full moon'. As the month progresses, we see different parts of the Moon's surface and these are known as 'phases'.

To begin, we have a period of darkness called the new moon, which is followed by the waxing crescent as the moon begins to emerge, forming a sliver, then a crescent shape. This is succeeded by the first quarter, and then the waxing gibbous as the lunar orb fills out, until eventually it becomes the full moon. From this point, the Moon begins to fade, passing into the waning gibbous, the third quarter and then the waning crescent. Slowly, it slips from sight and there is darkness once more. The period of around a week that leads up to the new moon is called the dark of the Moon.

As human beings, we have long been influenced by the power of the Moon and the pull of its tides. According to folklore and magical tradition, each moon phase has a specific energy that we can tap into:

THE NEW MOON

This is the time to set plans in motion, sow the seeds for the future and make a fresh start. New moons are the perfect phase to wipe the slate clean and move onto a new chapter in your life. Be bold and adventurous to make the most of this positive energy!

WAXING MOON

A waxing moon is the ideal time to build momentum, whether you're taking action towards a goal or expressing yourself in some other way, this lunar phase can help you move forwards and achieve success.

THE FULL MOON

The Moon is at the height of its power, making it a great time to step into your own power. Unleash your potential for all to see and express yourself fully. You'll be able to harness your intuition and imagination, so this is the ideal time to follow creative pursuits.

THE DARK OF THE MOON

This is a reflective phase and an ideal time to go within and seek answers. Your innate wisdom is in full flow and you'll be able to see the bigger picture when it comes to your life. This lunar phase can help you break habits and overcome obstacles.

MOON SIGNS

Your moon (or lunar) sign is the astrological sign where the Moon was at the moment of your birth. It casts light upon your inner world, revealing your emotional side and how you interact with others. In effect, it is the subconscious part of your identity and influences your dreams and desires. While the sun sign governs what we see on the surface, your lunar sign goes within to the heart of what matters, just like the Moon illuminates hidden parts of the landscape at night. There are many online tools that will help you calculate your moon sign; all you need is your date of birth and an idea of the time you were born. You will find information about each of the moon signs throughout this book:

JANUARY

FULL MOON NAME

WOLF MOON

As night falls and the new year dawns, an eerie symphony can be heard. It is the plaintive call of the wolves, an ethereal accompaniment to the icy mists that cloak the land. The howls are a call to arms and herald a new beginning – acknowledged by the ancient tribes through name of this full moon. They understood the power that is unleashed when you find your voice. As communal creatures, wolves share the load: they work together, all taking on different roles within the pack.

Consider how you can share the load this month. Express how you feel, and reach out to the wider community.

MONTHLY NEW MOON RITUAL

Tap into the inspiring energy of the new moon by setting some intentions. You can do this visually by creating a vision board outlining your goals for the months ahead.

You will need: journal, pen, pencils, large piece of paper, selection of magazines or other images, scissors, glue

· First, sit quietly with your left hand upon your heart. Close your eyes and let your mind wander.

· Think about areas of your life you'd like to improve and visualize the things you'd like to attract. Relax and let those images float through your mind.

· When you're ready, open your eyes. In your journal, write any thoughts, pictures or symbols that you can recall.

· Next, take a large sheet of paper. You will use this to create your vision board, so think about how you'd like it to look. This is your design, so lean into your intuition. You can experiment with different colours and shapes, as well as sketches or photos from magazines or newspapers.

· Fill the board with images, words and photos that represent how you feel and what you'd like to attract.

· Finally, place the vision board somewhere you'll see it every day and be reminded of your goals. The positive energy will help make your dreams a reality.

LUNAR ANIMAL FOR JANUARY

RABBIT

If you gaze at the Moon you might see the etched outline of a floppy-eared bunny upon its surface. Rabbits have a long association with all things lunar and feature in East Asian folklore.

According to the Japanese folk tale 'Tsuki no usagi', which means 'Moon Rabbit', the Man on the Moon came down to Earth disguised as a lowly beggar. He asked each of the animals for food, but while the fox brought him fish from the stream and the monkey fruit from the trees, little rabbit had nothing but grass to offer and so he told the beggar to build a fire. As the flames reached towards the heavens, the rabbit flung himself upon the pyre as an offering. The Man on the Moon's heart swelled with love at such a generous sacrifice, and he carried the rabbit into the night sky, where he remained glimmering from the surface of the Moon – a symbol of honour and sacrifice.

MONTHLY FULL MOON RITUAL

The enriching energy of a full moon can help you step into your power and feel rejuvenated. Focus on self-care during this full moon and practise a relaxing breathing exercise.

· Find a comfortable space where you can sit and be still. Choose a spot by a window, if you are able to, so that you can see the Moon in the sky.

· Set your intention by stating out loud:
'I allow myself to fully let go, in this moment.'

· Close your eyes and relax your body. Let your shoulders fall back, open your chest, and draw a deep breath in through your nose.

· As you do this, visualize the Moon glowing above you. Imagine that this breath is infused with lunar light and love.

· Exhale through your mouth, taking your time to expel all of the breath.

· Repeat the cycle for a couple of minutes, extending each inward and outward breath. Focus on drawing in the Moon's soothing energy through your body, into every muscle and bone.

JANUARY LUNAR FOOD

CABBAGE

This nutritious brassica, which is as easy to grow as it is to cook, is associated with both the Moon and the element of water – most likely because of its circular shape and many-layered appearance. White cabbage in particular was once considered sacred to the lunar orb and was picked, cooked and eaten on the evening of the full moon. Thought to hold protective powers, the cabbage was also linked to love and prosperity, and the leaves were used in rituals and spells to attract good fortune.

SPELL TO ATTRACT NEW LOVE

You will need: small white cabbage, knife, white yarn or ribbon

Cast this spell: when the Moon is waxing

· Chop the white cabbage in half.

· Speak the following words:
  'Two halves and one, my love will come.
  Together sweet when this I eat.'

· Bind the cabbage together with white yarn or ribbon, so the two separate halves become whole once more.

· The next day, chop both halves of the cabbage up and eat – raw in a salad, or boiled and added to a soup or stew.

· As you eat, repeat the magical chant.

SELENE

A serene and glowing beauty, Selene was a Titan and the Greek goddess of the Moon. A radiant being, draped in a gleaming cloak, she rode through the heavens on a chariot drawn by winged steeds, or by thundering oxen. Her crown was the crescent moon, which framed her flowing locks and made her appear even more beautiful against the velvety backdrop of the night.

She rode alone while her true love, Endymion, lay sleeping in a cave near the peak of the Lydian Mount Latmos. Endymion, a mortal shepherd, was gifted immortality by Zeus, and then cast into an eternal slumber, but that didn't sway Selene. Their nightly trysts produced many children, who became the twinkling stars alongside their mother's brightness.

SPELL FOR A SWEET DREAM PILLOW

Ensure you have a deep, dream-filled sleep, like Endymion, with a little help from the moon goddess Selene.

You will need: 2 handkerchiefs of equal size, needle and thread, bunch of dried lavender, polished moonstone tumble

· Sew the handkerchiefs together along three sides, leaving an opening to fill the bag.

· Fill with the lavender, associated with the Moon's soothing energy, and the moonstone, which has calming properties.

· Sew up the remaining edge and pop the bag beneath your regular pillow to promote a restful sleep.

SELENE

MOON SIGN OF THE MONTH

CAPRICORN

Calm and responsible, lunar Capricorns crave stability and order when it comes to everyday life. Their cool exterior can be seen as a safety mechanism against the chaos. Though they feel things deeply, they tend to keep a lid on their emotions and feel uncomfortable opening up. The truth is, they are just as sensitive as all of the other signs, even though they appear composed on the surface. This moon sign likes to feel useful to society and to make a contribution in some way. Reliable and trustworthy, the Moon in Capricorn makes a loyal companion and friend.

MOON SPELL TO RELEASE EMOTIONS

You will need: small piece of paper, ink pen, white thread, bowl filled with water, scissors

Cast this spell: when the Moon is waning

- To begin, sit quietly and place both hands over your heart. Breathe deeply and relax.

- Let any emotions rise to the surface and allow your thoughts to flow. Consider what is bothering you right now and how you feel.

- Note down a few sentences to describe your emotions. If there's something you'd like to get off your chest, take this opportunity to write it down.

- Roll the paper up into a scroll and tie with the thread.

- Hold the scroll over the bowl of water and say:
  'I let my words flow free, I express the truth of me. I let go and let it be.'

- Cut the thread that holds the paper in place and allow the paper to drop into the water.

- As the ink swirls and fades, repeat the magical chant.

FEBRUARY

FULL MOON NAME

SNOW MOON

Bitter is the biting wind as it meanders over hill and valley, bringing with it the full force of midwinter. There is no relief from the deathly cold, and those who worked the land knew this, which is why February's full moon is known as the Snow Moon, the Bone Moon and also the Ice Moon. Hunger was rife and, for many, deadly, so it also became known as the Hunger Moon. The extremes of nature were harsh, so those who faced them found succour in looking to the future, for as the wheel of the year turns, so too do the seasons, and lighter, brighter times come into view.

This Snow Moon, be assured that you, too, will prevail. Just like the ancients, you have the strength and resilience to deal with any obstacle in your path.

MONTHLY NEW MOON RITUAL

The new moon is a good time to wipe the slate clean and clear the clutter from your life. Physically tidying the space around you can provide clarity, giving you room to breathe and move forwards.

· Take a room and split it into two halves to make this task manageable. Spend an allotted amount of time clearing each side of the room.

· Look at your belongings with fresh eyes. Consider whether you really need them, if they have emotional attachment, or if they no longer serve a purpose.

· Be honest with yourself about what you need and what you can do without.

· Any items you don't want, parcel up for recycling.

· Enjoy relaxing in the space you have created.

CELTIC TRADITIONS

The Celtic druids placed significance on the shifting cycles of the Moon. Each new phase held power and potential, which was used for the benefit of the tribe. Seeds were sown during the waxing phase, in the hope that the Moon's growing form would encourage them to flourish. The wooden spars used to thatch roofs were similarly cut and crafted during waxing phases, in the hope that they'd be strengthened by the lunar rays, while a child born on a new moon was considered supremely blessed.

The waning moon was also thought to have healing benefits. Those that suffered from warts and sores would pray for relief, hoping that as the Moon faded so would their ailments. When the Moon was new, country folk would drop to their knees and make a wish for health and wealth. Some made the sign of the cross as they gazed upon the returning orb, believing its disappearance to be supernatural.

MONTHLY FULL MOON RITUAL

When the Moon is full, it is at the peak of its power. This is the perfect time to ask for help, particularly if you're struggling to break a habit or let something go. Let the cold season inspire you and put your problem on ice.

You will need: small piece of paper, pen, ice-cube tray or ice mould

· On the evening of the full moon, spend some time in a state of quiet reflection. Think of what you need help with and try to sum it up in a couple of words.

· It helps if you go to the root of the problem and think about any emotions associated with it. For example, if you'd like to quit an unhealthy habit, you might be feeling fearful and weak, so the words you come up with might be 'fear' and 'weakness'.

· Write the words down on a small piece of paper and scrunch it up into a tiny ball.

· Place this in the bottom of an ice-cube tray, then cover it with water.

· Pop the tray into the freezer and say:
'*I release the hold you have over me, I freeze your power, I am set free.*'

· When the next full moon comes around, remove the ice-cube tray from the freezer, place it outside and let the moonlight absorb the energy from the ice as it melts.

FEBRUARY LUNAR FOOD

COCONUT

With its smooth, milky white centre, cocooned by a globe of darkness, it's no surprise that the coconut is associated with the Moon. To the ancients, this simple fruit was a symbolic reminder of the lunar cycle, and how the dark of the Moon transforms to reveal the shining orb within. Thought to contain protective qualities, coconut shells were often stuffed with herbs and buried on the boundary of the home to keep evil at bay. In some cultures, coconuts are smashed in a ceremony intended to break barriers and eliminate negative energy.

SPELL FOR WHEN YOU'RE FEELING VULNERABLE

You will need: rice pudding, coconut milk, honey

Cast this spell: on a night when the Moon is waning

- First, make the rice pudding, either from scratch or by heating up a store-bought can.

- Pour two tablespoons of coconut milk over the pudding. As you do this, say:
  'May the light of the Moon be my cocoon.
  Nourish my soul and keep me whole.'

- Add a drizzle of honey (associated with love and self-care).

- Take your spoon and stir in a clockwise direction and repeat the magical chant.

- As you eat the pudding, visualize yourself cocooned in lunar light.

ARTEMIS

MOON DEITY

ARTEMIS

Artemis, the Greek goddess of wild animals and the hunt, was associated with all things lunar. She is said to have worn a crescent moon crown upon her head, as she stalked the forest. Governed by her instincts, Artemis was known for her intuition and the ability to see and hear the creatures of the night. Guided by the Moon's light, she could navigate the wild places, and always find her way home.

Most commonly seen parading through the undergrowth with her wood nymphs, she was known for her free spirit and skill as a huntress. Men and gods tried to woo her – including her fellow hunter Orion – but he, like all the rest, met his doom. Chaste and strong, Artemis vigorously protected her innocence, killing any who dared make advances.

SPELL FOR A NATURE CHARM

Connect with the nurturing energy of the natural world, through the power of Artemis.

You will need: a decorative bowl; an assortment of nature's gifts that you have foraged, such as stones and pebbles, flowers, seeds and fruit; pen and paper

- Fill the bowl with all of the items you've gathered.

- On the paper, draw a crescent moon – the symbol of Artemis – and place it beneath the bowl, then position it in the middle of your table.

- Make a wish for the healing energy of nature to flow through your life.

MOON SIGN OF THE MONTH

AQUARIUS

Lunar Aquarians often come across as aloof, but the reason for this detached behaviour is that they have set themselves a challenge. They do not want to be dragged down by pettiness, and prefer to remain cool-headed at all times. They care deeply about the environment and their community, and will take great interest in humanitarian issues, but when the problems are closer to home, they tend to back off. This sign is supremely independent and shares the belief that others should follow suit. In relationships, they tend to be open-minded and allow the other person a great deal of freedom. Despite their need for space, lunar Aquarians are deeply loyal and will take a stand for anyone who needs their help.

MOON SPELL TO BOOST PERSONAL POWER TO PROTECT YOURSELF

You will need: black candle, frankincense essential oil, matches, smoky quartz

Cast this spell: during the dark of the Moon

· Anoint the candle with a couple of drops of the frankincense essential oil, renowned for its uplifting properties. This will help you feel more powerful.

· Light the candle and hold the smoky quartz in both hands. This beautiful crystal amplifies energy and will boost your inner strength.

· Close your eyes and take a long, deep breath in through your nose. Imagine that you are drawing the dark protective cloak of the night sky around your shoulders. As you exhale, feel the warm, rejuvenating energy cocoon you.

· Continue to breathe in this way for a few minutes.

· When you're ready, open your eyes and let the candle burn down.

· Whenever you're feeling vulnerable, carry the quartz with you for protection.

SPRING

The subtle stirrings of spring can be felt beneath our feet as we walk. The gentle rumble of the belly of the Earth tickles our toes with the promise of potential, and, just like that, new shoots emerge into the lunar light, their sleepy heads bathed by moon rays. It is just the beginning, the start of a new adventure. This season is not unlike the new moon – it greets the dawn of a fresh cycle. Brimming with possibility, spring is a time to plant seeds and watch them grow. Ideas fall like moondust, scattering at our feet, and it is up to us to nurture each grain of light and embrace the magic. Anything is possible when the Moon and the Earth are in sync and spring has sprung.

MARCH

FULL MOON NAME

WORM MOON

The final full moon of winter is here, and so the Earth awakens. Beneath the icy crust, there is movement – at first, tiny: slithering, wriggling, as the worms begin their trail afresh. A new cycle has begun, and so to mark this change the Worm Moon is born. Also known as the Chaste Moon, for it brings a quickening to the Earth's layer, the Crust Moon and the Sap Moon. Slowly but surely the earth begins to thaw. There is possibility at its heart, and the potential for new life.

This full moon urges you to make plans: be ready to seize the moment, for it is coming! Let your ideas find their way to the surface, where they can be made real.

MONTHLY FULL MOON RITUAL

Trigger your imagination and unleash your inner artist this full moon.

Set some time aside to sit and take in the beauty of the Moon. Keep a sketch book, pen and any other 'crafty' tools by your side:

· Allow yourself the time to gaze at the Moon. Let your mind wander and do a spot of 'moon-dreaming'.

· You might experience a vision or see a stream of unrelated images. You'll likely feel a range of emotions or have random thoughts. Just enjoy delighting in the Moon's magic.

· If you feel the urge to draw, make notes or even write a poem, then do so. It doesn't have to be perfect; it's about allowing your artistic side free-rein. You may want to scribble down words or doodles as they come to you.

· What you do doesn't have to make sense. You're tapping into the Moon's creative energy and giving yourself the freedom to express yourself.

FOLKLORE AND SUPERSTITIONS

NATIVE AMERICAN TRADITIONS

To the Native Americans, the Moon was a guardian spirit, a watchful eye in the night sky; it shone and marked the passage of time. Its cycle was a way of counting the days and the seasons, and so the Moon became a friend who could not only light the way, but also promote new growth. They named each full moon depending on when it fell and the time of year, giving it significance and spiritual power.

Each tribe had their own Moon story: some revered its mystical energy, taking it as their clan symbol and carving it into totem poles; others honoured its mystery, believing it to be one of the most powerful beings in the universe. In one tale, the Moon is swallowed by a giant codfish and then regurgitated, when smoke from tribal fires causes a celestial coughing fit. In another, it is stolen, and then tossed into the river by the trickster Coyote. Each narrative is a nod to the Moon's continuous and ever-changing cycle.

MONTHLY NEW MOON RITUAL

Tap into the purifying power of a new moon and cleanse your aura of stagnant energy.

On the evening of a new moon, find a quiet spot where you can stand, breathe and check in with yourself.

- Stand with your feet hip-width apart, shoulders back, down and relaxed, and lengthen your spine.

- In your mind, picture a layer of light that extends outwards and surrounds your body.

- As you breathe in, imagine drawing the Moon's cleansing energy into this forcefield. See it as a white light that travels around your body, streaming through your aura and eliminating negative energy.

- When you exhale, imagine ridding your aura of any debris that has built up over the past year.

- Take your time and slow your breathing down. Continue to visualize the white light passing through your aura as you draw in each breath. Say:
  'I am filled with lunar light.'

MARCH LUNAR FOOD

PEPPERMINT

Although peppermint is associated with air, it's also considered a lunar herb as it is linked to the element of water. In Greek mythology, the water nymph Minthe was transformed into this plant by the goddess Persephone, who was jealous of her husband Pluto's love for the young maid. While she could never be released from the soily grasp of the land, she grew sweet-smelling, making her one of the most distinctive and magical herbs. Often planted by the entrance to the home to protect it from evil, mint was used in spells to enhance psychic ability, promote visions and attract love.

SPELL FOR LIFTING THE SPIRITS

You will need: small cup and saucer, hot water, peppermint essential oil, some dried peppermint leaves

- Half fill the cup with hot water, then add 6 drops of peppermint essential oil. This potent extract harnesses the energizing powers of the herb.

- Sprinkle the dried peppermint in a circle around the saucer to represent the Moon when it is full.

- Close your eyes and inhale the fresh aroma.

- Draw the scent down into your chest and stomach. As you do, ask the Moon to lift your mood.

MOON DEITY

MANI

Mani was the Norse lunar deity associated with reflection and protection. He rode across the sky in his gleaming chariot: while his sister Sunna, the sun, burst through the heavens during daylight hours, it was Mani who took centre-stage when darkness fell. The Vikings believed that the siblings worked together, commanding the ethereal realm and controlling the movement of time.

Mani was thought to be the polar opposite of his golden-haired sister, with pale, luminescent skin and raven-black hair to match the night sky. Often petitioned for strength and healing, he had a calming energy and was less of a warrior than some of his other-worldly counterparts.

SPELL FOR A HARMONY BRAID

Strengthen your friendships and boost those feel-good vibes with Mani's magical help.

You will need: three pieces of coloured yarn

- Braid the yarn together, interlacing the three coloured pieces to create a plait-like effect. Tie a knot at one end.

- Wrap the braid around your wrist, then knot together to create a loose circular bracelet to represent the Moon.

- As you do this, say:
  'I tie this knot, I seal the end.
  May harmony flow between me and my friend.'

- Gift the bracelet to a friend to strengthen the bond between you.

))) ● MANI ● (((

MOON SIGN OF THE MONTH

PISCES

'Dreamy' is how many might describe the lunar Pisces. These sweet-natured characters appear to have their head in the clouds, but that is only because they are highly intuitive. This moon sign finds it easy to empathize with people: they're compassionate and sensitive, and will often pick up on subtle shifts in energy and mood. Their sixth sense leaves them open to extreme emotions, and they may need to retreat, to detach themselves from situations that drain their spirit. Good-natured in most things, the lunar Pisces has a childish sense of fun, and can be the life and soul of the party.

SPELL TO TAKE BOLD ACTION AND BOOST COURAGE

You will need: bath tub, Epsom salts, crystals, shells, white petals

Cast this spell: when the Moon is waxing

· Run a warm bath, and add in a scoop of Epsom salts to cleanse and strengthen your aura.

· Arrange the crystals and shells around the bath tub and scatter the white petals on the surface of the water to help you connect with lunar energy.

· Immerse yourself slowly and relax.

· Imagine a dome of white light that comes to its apex over the bath.

· Take a deep breath and gently submerge yourself under the water for a couple of seconds. As you emerge, say: *'I am strong and ready to make my mark!'*

· Imagine you are covered from head to toe in silver armour.

APRIL

FULL MOON NAME

PINK MOON

Named after the wild phlox plant, a rosy bloom that spreads like a blanket over grassy meadows in North America, the Pink Moon heralds the arrival of spring and brings with it a wave of youthful energy. Warmth returns to the earth and tentatively turns up the brightness. The landscape sheds its faded hues and steps into the light once more, as spring flowers gently blossom. Also known as the Sprouting Grass Moon, the Egg Moon and the Hare Moon.

This full moon is synonymous with renewal. It's time to step into the light. Embrace the magic of the changing seasons and recognize the beauty in your own world.

MONTHLY NEW MOON RITUAL

Just like the Moon, you go through phases. There will be days when you can't help but shine, yet on other days you will want to retreat and take a moment for yourself. Honour your changing moods during this new moon by taking the time to check in with yourself and how you are feeling. This will help you clear your mind so that you have the space to grow and nurture new ideas.

· Be in the moment and engage your senses.

· How do you feel right now? What is on your mind?

· Spend some time writing down your thoughts and feelings.

· Accept and acknowledge them.

- You might want to make a statement or affirmation, such as:
  'I embrace and acknowledge how I feel in this moment.'
- Know that you are perfect as you are, right now.

SLAVIC TRADITIONS AND FOLKLORE

According to the Slavic tradition, the Moon is the primary object of worship in the sky, taking precedence over the sun and the stars. Supremely powerful, it has the ability to bestow good health and abundance upon those who honour it. From prayers and rituals to circular dances under the light of the full moon, there are many ways to petition its grace.

During a lunar eclipse, weapons were unleashed and fired towards the heavens in the hope that they might slaughter the beast who has the orb within its jaws. The people would show their dismay by weeping and wailing at the Moon's fate. Luckily this did not last long, for the Moon was swiftly released back into its heavenly home. In most Slavic folk tales, the Moon was considered male and called 'father' or 'grandfather', while in Bulgaria, it was customary to hail the moon *'Dedo Bozhe, Dedo Gospod'*, meaning 'Uncle God, Uncle Lord'.

MONTHLY FULL MOON RITUAL

Embrace feminine power and balance your emotions by creating a moon altar in your home.

- Clear a coffee table or a shelf of clutter, then think about how you'd like to dress the area. Use your intuition. If it's a table, you might want to cover it with a dark tablecloth to represent the night sky. If you have any images of the Moon or moon-inspired ornaments, you could display these.

- Next, think about crystals and stones that you can include: quartz, moonstone and obsidian are all good choices.

- A white candle or tealights can also be used to represent the Moon.

- Include a vase of your favourite white blooms, or a selection of lunar herbs, such as rosemary, lavender or mint.

- To finish, spend some time sitting near your altar and think about what the Moon means to you. Use this time to reflect on how you feel and what you would like for the future. Write down any wishes or musings and leave them in a dish on your altar.

APRIL LUNAR FOOD

POTATO

This hearty root vegetable was a diet staple for the ancients, and was also associated with the Moon's power, partly because of its size and roundish shape, but also because of the way it grew. It was auspicious to plant a crop shortly after a full moon, during the waning phase, and any potatoes grown during this time were thought to flourish. We now know that as the moonlight diminishes, so too does the level of moisture, which causes a below-ground growth spurt.

SPELL TO HELP YOU RELEASE STRESS

You will need: small potato, potato peeler or knife, soil

Cast this spell: the night after a full moon

· Hold the potato in both hands and bring to mind anything that is causing you anxiety.

· Try not to dwell on the issue, instead imagine pouring all of that negative energy into the skin of the potato.

· Next, scrape away the skin. It doesn't matter if it falls in pieces, or one continuous loop. Continue to peel until all of the skin is gone.

· As you shed the outer layer, imagine that you're also shedding the stress from your life.

· Gather up the peelings and bury them in the soil (either in a pot or on the ground).

· Cook the potato any way that you'd like. As you eat, give thanks for its nourishing power.

MOON DEITY

JACI

Known as the 'Mother of All' in Tupi-Guarani mythology, Jaci is the beautiful Brazilian moon goddess, and protectress of the night sky. With a deep love for her surroundings, she governs the plants and animals of the Amazon, keeping a watchful eye on them when darkness falls.

According to legend, she fell deeply in love with the sun god, Guaraci. He burned with passion for her, setting fire to the rainforest and beginning to consume the land. Jaci cried in anguish at the destruction and her tears quelled the flames. The lovers made a pact that they could never be together for the sake of their people, but Jaci was heartbroken. As her tears fell one final time, they formed the Amazon river.

SPELL FOR A LUNAR BEAUTY POTION

Unleash your radiance with this magical potion inspired by the beauty of the Amazon.

You will need: fresh water, small jug, pink rose petals, vanilla essential oil, funnel and small sieve, small spray bottle

- Boil the fresh water and half fill a small jug with it.
- Add the rose petals and a couple of drops of vanilla essential oil.
- Let the petals and the oil infuse the water for 5 minutes.
- Strain the liquid into a small spray bottle.
- Spritz lightly over your face and body. Say:
  'I let my light shine!'

JACI

MOON SIGN OF THE MONTH

ARIES

The lunar Aries likes to live in the moment and seize the day. Emotions bubble to the surface and can turn to frustration when the lunar Aries tries to express how they're feeling. Independent – and somewhat fiery – when the Moon sits in this sign you can expect plenty of passion. The combination of action-led Aries, with sensitive moon energy, makes for an interesting life, and this individual has a tendency to take things personally. That said, there's a sweetness in the way they approach life, and their emotional honesty means you'll always know where you stand and what they want from you.

MOON SPELL TO TAP INTO YOUR INTUITION

You will need: a few sheets of paper, pencil

Cast this spell: when the Moon is waning

· Take a sheet of paper and draw a circle in the centre.

· Write down any problems that you need help with in the circle.

· If there are issues that bother you, write a few words to sum them up.

· Fold the paper three times to represent the new moon, the full moon and the dark of the moon.

· Pop the paper beneath your pillow before bed time.

· Say the following:
'*Upon this night, while I rest in bed, let intuition fill my head. Bring me answers, insights deep, Mother Moon, while I'm asleep.*'

· Keep the remaining paper by your bedside and write down any visions or insights that you receive in your dreams.

MAY

FULL MOON NAME

FLOWER MOON

The delicate sweetness of spring blossom dances lightly upon the breeze, a gentle reminder that May has arrived, and with it the Flower Moon. Named after the pretty blooms that burst from the branches and litter the meadows, this full moon is also called the Milk Moon, an Anglo-Saxon term, and the Corn Planting Moon, a nod to the freshly planted crops.

The flowers of the field turn their faces to the sun; like them, we too can flourish. Use this phase to consider what you need to truly blossom.

MONTHLY FULL MOON RITUAL

Generate more positive energy by giving thanks for your blessings this full moon.

You will need: journal and pen

- Spend some time in quiet reflection by the light of the Moon.

- Breathe deeply, relax, and let the lunar rays illuminate your mind.

- Close your eyes and think of all the things for which you are grateful. Start by thinking about your day and the little things that have happened that made you smile, then build upon this by reviewing events from the previous week.

- Let those joyful thoughts linger in your mind. When you're ready, begin writing a list of your blessings.

- When you've finished, read through the list and recall the emotions associated with each gift.

- To finish, look at the Moon and say:
  'Every blessing fills my life with light and love.'

- Write down any wishes or musings and leave them in a dish on your altar.

FOLKLORE AND SUPERSTITIONS

MOON SUPERSTITIONS

There are many superstitions associated with the Moon. Hanging like a jewel in the night sky, to the ancients it must have seemed like a sign from the gods. The new moon was considered particularly fortuitous, and newborn babes were exposed to its rays in the hope that they would grow strong and be imbued with good health. Those who settled into a new home or cemented their nuptials during this time could also feel the benefit. It was thought that, as the Moon waxed, so too would their fortunes.

A full moon that falls on the 'moon's day', meaning Monday, was thought to be extremely lucky. If you were to gaze upon the orb unencumbered by wild shrubbery, you were indeed blessed, but look through the branches of a tree and it was a different story – this was considered an ill omen and to be avoided at all costs.

MONTHLY NEW MOON RITUAL

Open your mind to new possibilities by flexing your body in a series of lunar-inspired stretches.

· Create a relaxing environment by burning lavender oil or scented candles, and make sure you have plenty of room to flex and stretch. Stand with your feet hip-width apart, take a deep breath in and stretch your arms above your head. Feel the gentle pull of your spine as it lengthens.

· As you exhale, slowly curve your arms and hands forward, as if you're about to dive into the space in front of you. As you do this, bend from the waist to create a gentle arc, to represent the crescent moon.

· Hold this position for a few seconds as you breathe and think about the power of the crescent moon, then gently unfurl to a standing position, with your arms by your side.

· Take another long breath and this time when you raise your arms upwards, bring them out to the side as if you're painting a circle around you, to represent the full moon.

· As you exhale bring your arms down to the side, relax and think about the power and potential of this moon, and what it means for you.

MILK

Traditionally, milk was synonymous with feminine power and, like the Moon, it was considered gentle and nurturing, a gift given to the young to help them grow strong. The full moon in May is often called a Milk Moon, because it is the time of year that cattle and sheep fill their bellies with grass, ready to produce their flow. Milk, like the surface of the Moon, is white and creamy, imbued with light and life-giving energy. To the ancients, it was a magical elixir, as mysterious as the fluid radiance of the Moon.

SPELL TO HELP BOOST SELF-ESTEEM

You will need: warm bath, small glass of milk, honey

Cast this spell: during a waxing moon

· Run a bath. While you wait, take the glass of milk and stir in a spoonful of honey. Honey has nurturing properties, while the milk is imbued with healing lunar energy.

· Stir the mixture in a clockwise direction until all the honey has dissolved.

· When the bath is full, add the milky elixir to the water, and swirl with your hands.

· Immerse yourself in the water, close your eyes and imagine that you're bathed from head to toe in lunar light.

· Repeat in your head or out loud:
  'I let my light shine with love.'

MOON DEITY

ARIANRHOD

This beautiful Celtic goddess is associated with the Moon, fertility and the weaving of fate. Her name means 'Silver Wheel' and refers to both the changing cycles of life and her ability to determine destiny. From her revolving castle in the sky, known as Caer Sidi, she awaited the souls of the dead. Here, in what was thought to be the Celtic otherworld, she would offer respite, while considering their ultimate end.

A free spirit who no-one could tame, she had many loves, including a merman. Her association with water runs deep, and her ability to nourish the soul and offer rejuvenation was celebrated. When her followers needed to call on her, they would look to the North Star and the Moon for guidance.

SPELL FOR THE STAR OF HOPE

Look to the future with optimism and joy by weaving a path through the stars.

You will need: handful of white tealights, pen and paper, matches

· Arrange the tealights into the shape of a star. On the paper, write the word 'hope' in big letters. Reflect for a moment – what would bring you hope right now?

· Position the paper in the centre of the tealight star.

· Light the tealights and say:
 'As the North Star shines up in the sky, I am filled with hope, my spirits are high.'

· Let the tealights burn down.

ARIANRHOD

MOON SIGN OF THE MONTH

TAURUS

Calm and steadfast, the lunar Taurus is grounded and has a trusted circle of loyal friends. There's a serene quality to these individuals, and they will go out of their way to avoid overt displays of emotion or sudden outbursts. While they enjoy the luxuries in life, home comforts always come first, as this is the place where they feel most secure. Those with a Taurus moon sign can be relied on when the going gets tough, but while their dependable nature makes them good friends and confidants, others might suggest they are stuck in their ways. Lunar bulls may be stubborn, but when it comes to love they are constant and faithful companions. They'll always put their partner first and will never waver in their commitment.

MOON SPELL TO SOOTHE YOUR SOUL

You will need: moonstone, pot, 2 glasses, water

Cast this spell: during any moon phase

· Sit beneath the light of the Moon. If it's warm, you might choose to do this outside, but by a window is fine.

· Gaze up at the Moon and take in its beauty. It doesn't matter what shape it is, the Moon always illuminates, and even during the dark phase of the Moon it is present.

· Place the moonstone in a clean pot beneath its light.

· Make a wish for the Moon to imbue the stone with soothing energy.

· Leave the stone overnight.

· In the morning, place the stone in a glass and cover with fresh water for a few minutes.

· Decant the water into a fresh glass and sip slowly.

· Let the calming lunar energy fill you up.

· Keep the moonstone with you as a healing charm.

SUMMER

Summer parades its colours with pride, bathing the landscape in a rainbow glow. She dances merrily through the fields and meadows, and with a flick of her wand turns up the heat, but it is at night that we see her true power. In the lilting shadows of the evening, as the Moon takes centre stage, summer truly sparkles. Like a moon in full swell at the pinnacle of its cycle, she is ready. Nothing can stand in her way, and as we watch from our earthly seat, we too step into the lunar shine, throw our arms wide and say, *'Mother Moon, you are divine!'* For if we can tap into the potential of the season, and the energy of this mystical orb, we can do anything!

JUNE

FULL MOON NAME

STRAWBERRY MOON

June make its entrance, bringing with it the plumpest of fruit, ripe and ready to pick, but only for the shortest time, and so this month's full moon is the aptly named Strawberry Moon. Those early tribes took advantage of this moment and of the glorious sweetness of nature's gift. They learned to seize such opportunities, for they were like jewels, a rich reward for all their struggles earlier in the year.

This full moon asks you to look for the sweetness in times of trouble, to think of problems as gifts, and to let opportunities evolve.

MONTHLY FULL MOON RITUAL

Connect with the flow of lunar energy, by taking a mindful walk with a loved one under the light of the full moon.

- Wait with your friend until the Moon is full in the sky. Spend a few minutes appreciating its beauty together.

- Take your time and don't rush the experience. A gentle meander in the outdoors beneath the light of the full moon should be savoured.

- Breathe deeply as you stroll and engage your senses. Don't be afraid to walk in silence with each other.

- Consider what you can see and how the landscape looks different in the moonlight. Discuss with your friend – did they spot something you didn't?

- Think about what you can hear – the sound of the night, from the thick veil of silence to the gentle rustle of creatures – has a melody all of its own. Breathe in this music and let it touch your soul.

- Consider what you both can smell and feel, and how the Moon accentuates this.

- Reach out and touch the ground, feel it beneath your feet and listen to the movements you and your friend make in the darkness.

- Enjoy the experience and let it fill you with wonder.

FOLKLORE AND SUPERSTITIONS

AFRICAN MOON MYTHS

In Africa, the Moon is a symbol of feminine power and strength. Associated with the essence of life, it was revered by the ancients, because of the lunar impact upon the Earth and agriculture. Moon myths vary, depending on the tribe, and there are many tales that outline the creation of the lunar orb.

One folktale describes how the Sun and Moon once lived upon the Earth as man and wife. The Sun built his house upon the land but failed to make it big enough to encompass his light, so when the water came to visit, both he and his lunar wife were driven into the sky. Another tale suggests that there were two suns, who were rivals. They agreed that they would jump into the water, and one would live upstream from the other. Instead of doing this fairly, one sun tricked the other into jumping first. The water depletes his shine, and he becomes the Moon.

MONTHLY NEW MOON RITUAL

Appreciate friends and family and tap into your innate creativity with this ritual.

You will need: large sheet of dark paper, silver pen, glue, glitter

- Imagine yourself as the Moon, vibrant and glowing in the sky. Inhale and visualize this clearly in your mind.

- Visualize the stars that surround you. These are your friends and family, the people who keep you company upon this earthly journey.

- Draw the Moon in the centre of the paper, then add a halo of stars to represent each one of your friends and family.

- Think of friends and relatives you haven't seen for a while. Position these somewhere in the sky looking down on you.

- Consider colleagues and acquaintances, people who are potential friends, and put them in the picture too.

- Be creative and scatter glitter to create a beautiful collage of the night.

- When you've finished, look at the picture and acknowledge the wonderful support network of stars in your life.

JUNE LUNAR FOOD

KAVA

This bushy shrub, which thrives in the shade and prefers the moist loose soil of the Pacific Islands, is associated with the Moon because of its watery influence. A fan of rainfall, the kava plant (sometimes known as kava kava) flourishes in a damp environment. Over the years, it has become a key ingredient in many recipes and is known for its calming properties. It can alleviate anxiety and also combat insomnia, making it a popular ingredient in lunar spells to soothe the body and mind.

SPELL FOR A RESTFUL NIGHT'S SLEEP

You will need: kava root powder, honey, almond milk, ice, blender, glass, white candle, matches

Cast this spell: during the waning moon phase

· Add a teaspoon of kava root powder and a teaspoon of honey to a blender, then pour in a small glass of almond milk and add a handful of ice. Honey is considered nurturing and almond milk is associated with lunar energy.

· Blend together until smooth.

· Decant into a glass.

· Light the candle and spend a few minutes gazing into the flame. Breathe deeply and focus on the light – this will help to quieten your mind as you sip the drink.

· Imagine the Moon's light as a soft blanket. Feel it wrap around your shoulders and support you, as you watch the candle burn.

MOON DEITY

THOTH

The Egyptian god Thoth is associated with writing, magic and the Moon. Known as a mild-mannered mediator among the other deities, he was often called upon to settle scores and negotiate. The goddess Nut was cursed by her father Ra not to give birth on any day of the year. She sought Thoth's help, who made a bet with the Moon to win five extra days in the year so that Nut could give birth to her children. In doing so, he changed the annual calendar from 360 to 365 days, shaping time and becoming a patron of order and justice. Thoth invented language and the gift of writing.

SPELL FOR THE POEM POWER

Make your wishes come true by harnessing your inner wordsmith, with a little help from Thoth.

You will need: white candle, matches, pen and paper, teaspoon

· Light the candle and decide on a wish. Gaze into the flame and ask the Moon for inspiration.

· Turn your wish into a simple rhyme, for example:
  'I wish for love, from up above.
  To take a chance on new romance.'

· Write the words on the paper and finish with:
  'As I see, so it will be.'

· Fold the paper into a scroll. Use the spoon to scoop up a small amount of soft wax from the top of the candle, then use this to seal your pledge.

· Leave the scroll beneath the light of the Moon for 5 days.

THOTH

MOON SIGN OF THE MONTH

GEMINI

Those with a Gemini moon sign are likely to be curious and interested in everything. They love to learn and are constantly intrigued by life and its mysteries. With their lunar influence being mutable and airy, they will flit from one thing to another and have lots of projects on the go. Chatty and sociable, the lunar Gemini finds it easy to mix with people and loves talking, but while their outward appearance is gregarious, inside they can often feel unsettled. This sign sometimes struggles with anxiety and has a nervous disposition, although they hide it well. In relationships, they are fun and spontaneous, although they do get restless at times. They like to be open and talk about their feelings.

MOON SPELL TO EXPAND YOUR MIND

You will need: handful of small stones, pomegranate seeds

Cast this spell: a few days before or on a full moon

- Stand outside barefoot on the grass beneath the light of the Moon.

- Arrange the stones in a circle to represent a full moon, then stand in the centre.

- Take the pomegranate seeds in both hands and say:
  'These seeds I sow, please let them grow.
  Ignite my mind until I find the light within to help me win.'

- Spin around and scatter the seeds into the wind.

- Imagine an orb of white light resting in the space behind your eyes. It sheds light and provides inspiration for all your endeavours.

JULY

FULL MOON NAME

BUCK MOON

The generous warmth of the sun brightens the landscape and the earth responds – it is bristling with life and energy. The young bucks that have come into adulthood are primed and ready. As the lunar orb reaches fullness, their antlers emerge and so the Buck Moon takes its name and place in the night sky. Also called the Thunder Moon because of the abundance of thunderstorms that occur during this month, the undercurrent of power is strong.

It is time to embrace your calling, step outside and engage with your surroundings. Let nature and the wonder of the Moon excite you!

MONTHLY NEW MOON RITUAL

Wipe the slate clean with a simple meditation that harnesses the rejuvenating power of the new moon.

· If you can, find a quiet spot outside and sit on the ground.

· Press your body into the earth and feel your connection with the natural world.

· Close your eyes and breathe deeply.

· Imagine you are looking out on a clear vista, a valley of green meadows and blue skies. Focus on this image and the empty space before you.

· You can go anywhere and do anything; you can be anyone you choose to be in this space. You are the first person to venture onto this land.

· Breathe and relax.

· Feel the blanket of opportunity that is laid before you. Know that, at this point, you have the power to create your future.

· When you're ready, open your eyes, give your limbs a shake and smile.

FOLKLORE AND SUPERSTITIONS

INUIT MOON MYTHS

The Inuit people believed that the Sun and the Moon were siblings. The Sun was called Malina and the Moon, Anningan. As children, they would play together in the shadows, until one fateful night, Anningan assaulted his sister. The struggle that ensued caused an oil lamp to break. Malina's hands were covered in grease, which she rubbed upon her brother's face, causing it to blacken in patches. In anguish, she fled to the sky, with her brother in hot pursuit. There they became the Sun and Moon and were forever bound in a cosmic chase through the heavens.

According to the Inuit legend, the Moon was so obsessed with his sister that he would forget to eat. As the nights slipped by, he would become thinner and thinner until eventually he wasted away, disappearing from the sky for three nights. But he would always reappear, renewed and ready for the chase once more.

MONTHLY FULL MOON RITUAL

Embrace the nurturing energy of a full moon and treat yourself with love by cooking a delicious meal from scratch.

You will need: simple recipe (such as for a stew or soup), the ingredients, some candles, matches, flowers

· Set aside plenty of time, so that you can prepare and cook your meal and make it an event.

· Put love and energy into everything you do, so chop, blend and stir with the intention of making a delicious meal for yourself.

· As you add ingredients, think about their goodness and how they will help to nourish you.

· Be mindful and present. Engage with the experience.

· When the meal is ready, set the table with love. Imagine you're taking yourself on a romantic date and dress the table with candles and flower.

· Take your time and enjoy the meal. Savour each mouthful and give thanks for this tasty treat.

· Enjoy the experience and let it fill you with wonder.

WATERCRESS

Packed with nutrients, watercress is a medicinal powerhouse, but its magic doesn't end there. In folklore, it was associated with the Moon, mainly because of its aquatic nature. Any plant linked to water was thought to be imbued with lunar energy. As such, watercress was highly protective while also being a popular choice in spells for psychic power and prophetic visions. It was also used as a charm to keep those who were travelling over the sea safe.

SPELL FOR IMPROVING INTUITION

You will need: handful of fresh watercress, 2 bowls, hot water, sieve, some ink

Cast this spell: when the Moon is waning

· Place the bundle of watercress into a bowl of hot water and let it steep for 5 minutes.

· Strain the liquid into another bowl, then add 3–4 drops of ink to the water and swirl in a clockwise direction.

· Close your eyes. Spend a couple of minutes breathing deeply to clear your mind. When you're ready, open your eyes and look into the water. Let your gaze soften and continue to take long, slow breaths.

· You may notice strange patterns, letters and symbols floating upon the surface. Don't try to make sense of them; simply pay attention to your thoughts and emotions.

· Make a note of any impressions that stay with you, as these may be intuitive messages from your subconscious.

MOON DEITY

IX CHEL

This Mayan goddess of the Moon was supremely powerful, and associated with fertility and destiny. She had the ability to change shape and could appear as a beautiful young maiden with a beak for her upper lip, or sometimes a wise old crone with a serpent crown, a gaping mouth and claws for hands and feet. In this form, she was considered her most magnificent, but also merciless, with the ability to summon the rain and bring floods. The rainbow was one of her many symbols, along with an overturned jar. A physician goddess, Ix Chel was called upon during childbirth to undertake the role of heavenly midwife and provide strength and support.

SPELL FOR THE RAINBOW RICHES

Boost prosperity by using one of Ix Chel's famous symbols along with a powerful visualization.

You will need: a shower and some time to visualize

Cast this spell: when the Moon is waxing

· Stand beneath the shower, close your eyes and visualize a rainbow above your head: the vibrant colours of the arc flow down to greet you, hitting the top of your head and cascading over your body, shimmering with coloured light.

· Continue to visualize this image. Feel the warmth of the rainbow rays as they're absorbed into your skin.

· Say in your head:
   *'By the power of the rainbow, and the magic of the Moon,
   I am open and ready for a financial boon.'*

IXCHEL

MOON SIGN OF THE MONTH

CANCER

The Moon is at home in Cancer, making this one of the most emotional lunar positions. People with this moon sign are highly sensitive and intuitive to the moods of others. That said, they can be easily consumed by their own emotions and have a tendency to dwell upon the past. When they're hurt, they take it to heart and may find it difficult to forgive, but that doesn't mean they'll confront their aggressor. These gentle souls prefer to keep the peace and often bottle things up. They like to feel secure in their relationships, and that goes for friendships, too, but when treated with kindness, they will return the favour. Dependable and generous, you can expect to feel the love when in their company.

MOON SPELL TO BOOST YOUR EMOTIONAL STRENGTH

You will need: quartz crystal, black scarf

Cast this spell: any time during or after the new moon phase

· This spell works over two evenings. On the first evening, place your quartz crystal outside, beneath the light of the Moon. Smoky quartz will provide protection and grounding.

· Leave the stone to absorb those powerful lunar rays.

· Retrieve the stone the next day and wrap in a black scarf to protect it.

· That evening, take the quartz and hold it over the centre of your chest, where your heart chakra resides. This is the energy centre associated with your emotions.

· Close your eyes, breathe deeply and imagine you are absorbing the powerful energy of the stone.

· Quartz is a natural magnifier, which means any lunar rays are enhanced.

· Spend a couple of minutes breathing in the stone's energy.

AUGUST

FULL MOON NAME

STURGEON MOON

A symbol of longevity, sturgeon were abundant in the Great Lakes of North America in the month of August. The teeming rivers were full of silvery swathes, which offered a rich supply of nourishment for those first tribes, and so they marked this blessing by giving the full moon this fishy moniker. Also known as the Green Corn Moon, the Grain Moon and the Red Moon, after the burning glow of late summer evenings.

This full moon is a time to embrace the abundance in your world. What makes you feel rich, and how can you share this blessing with others?

MONTHLY FULL MOON RITUAL

Boost personal power by creating a full moon affirmation that will attract positive energy.

- If possible, do this ritual outside beneath the light of the Moon.

- Find a spot where you can sit and simply gaze up at the night sky. Take in its beauty and let the lunar light infuse you with energy.

- Draw upon the power of stillness as you breathe.

- When you're ready, think about words that make you feel strong. Write a list, then pick out the ones that call to you, for example 'vibrant' or 'powerful'.

- If you're struggling to think of anything, look up at the Moon and ask for guidance.

- Put the words into an affirmation set in the present, so you might say, 'I am vibrant and powerful', or, 'My vibrant power shines with every breath I take.'

- Repeat this aloud and see how it feels. Put emotion into it and say the words with feeling.

- Repeat the affirmation at least once a day, until the next full moon.

FOLKLORE AND SUPERSTITIONS

THE MOON AND THE TIDES

The Moon's connection to the tides on Earth are a subject of much speculation and folklore. One Maori myth tells the story of Rona, the beautiful daughter of the sea god Tangaroa. Known as 'Tide Collector', it was her job to gather and control the flow of water from the ocean. One night, she was carrying her water bucket home. It was late and the path was dark and cloaked in shadow. The Moon had slipped behind the clouds and Rona struggled to see anything. She caught her foot against a rock and in a fit of anger cursed the lack of lunar light. The Moon was incensed by her harsh words and decided to punish the Maori people. He seized Rona and her water bucket and carried her off into the night sky. It is believed that on days when Rona is unhappy, she flips the bucket upside down, and the Earth is drenched in rainfall.

MONTHLY NEW MOON RITUAL

Celebrate your wins this new moon: this ritual will help you to attract even more success!

· Light a candle and set the scene for a celebration.

· You might want to put on some music, dress up and pour yourself your favourite drink.

· Spend some time thinking about all the little things you've achieved so far this week. Small wins count, so whether it's a simple victory like finding a car parking space, or something bigger, like achieving a fitness goal, it doesn't matter.

· Make a list of your successes, no matter how big or small they may seem.

· If you're struggling, widen the parameters and think about the last few months, or even review the year.

· Once you have your list, read it and marvel at all the things you've done.

· Raise a glass and make a toast to your brilliance, then stick the list somewhere that you can see it every day – in a diary, on your altar or even on your fridge!

BREAD

A diet staple of the ancients, bread provided sustenance and strength, and was associated with health and abundance. Breaking bread has long been a tradition between friends and neighbours to cement relationships and promote wellbeing. White bread, in particular, is linked to the Moon and infused with lunar power. Associated with the Egyptian goddess Isis, who also governs the Moon, bread can be used in rites and rituals for grounding and to attract positive energy.

SPELL FOR IMPROVING INTUITION

You will need: a couple of slices of white bread, small bowl, outdoor space

Cast this spell: at night when the moon is waxing

· Break the bread into lots of tiny pieces in the bowl.

· Run your fingers through the crumbs. Think of all of the thousands of opportunities that come your way during your lifetime.

· Go outside and gaze up at the Moon. During its waxing phase, it is building power and constantly changing shape.

· Scoop up a handful of the crumbs and scatter in a circle around you. Say:
  'May the crumbs of opportunity fall at my feet and nourish my life.'

· Continue to scatter the bread in a clockwise circle to attract positive energy.

MOON DEITY

CHANDRA

This Hindu god from the Vedic tradition was associated with the Moon and with plant life. He governed the night sky, soaring through the heavens on a chariot pulled by an antelope. With skin as white as snow, he was a ghostly vision, often depicted wielding a mace or carrying a lotus flower.

Chandra was married to 27 sisters, but favoured one over the others. The scorned wives complained to their father, who cast a spell to make Chandra's lunar light wane each month. In remorse, Chandra sought the help of the great god Shiva. He made the Moon also wax and grow in strength.

SPELL FOR THE LUNAR LOTUS

Promote inner peace with this simple healing spell.

You will need: white candle, white scarf, white flower, jar, water, candle, matches

· Light the candle to represent the Moon's light. Use the scarf to create a circle around the candle, from a safe distance.

· Hold the flower, which represents Chandra's lotus, in both hands. Say:
'Lotus of peace, let your soothing energy fill my heart and mind. I breathe in peace; I breathe out peace. I am peace.'

· Place the flower in some water on a sill beneath the light of the Moon.

· Take the scarf and wrap it around your head and neck. Close your eyes and breathe deeply.

· Whenever you need to feel calm, simply put on the scarf.

CHANDRA

MOON SIGN OF THE MONTH

LEO

Lunar Leos adore the spotlight, particularly if they're with close friends and family. They like to hold court and provide the entertainment. Charming and creative, they can be bossy at times, and enjoy taking control in most situations. That's not to say that they don't appreciate their nearest and dearest, they just have an innate need to organize everyone. Love is what really makes them tick, and they like to be nurtured. If they feel slighted, then their emotions will flare and you can guarantee drama – but only in private: they don't like to tarnish their sunny image. Renowned for their integrity, you can count on the Leo moon sign to be honest and fair in all things.

MOON SPELL TO FIND YOUR BALANCE

You will need: a white and a black candle of roughly the same size, pin, matches

Cast this spell: during the waning crescent moon

· Take each candle and carve a half moon shape into the wax using the pin. On one, ensure the Moon is curved to the right and on the other curved to the left, so that if you put them together they make a full moon.

· Place the candles next to each other and light them.

· Gaze at the flames and breathe deeply. Feel your body and mind relax.

· Take a long deep breath in. As you exhale, say:
'With every breath I take, my inner and outer self unite, I am in perfect balance.'

· Watch the candles burn down and continue to inhale and exhale deeply.

AUTUMN

Autumn burns sweet and low, her amber glow a tiny flame cast towards the Earth. She does not storm the land with ardour but is a gentle invader offering time to reflect. She does not want to steal the show, and yet the colours she brings are worthy of any prize. And like the vibrant hues that crinkle beneath our feet, so too does the Moon curl into a glistening crown, a crescent that sits easily upon the autumn breeze. It nestles in the night sky and says, 'Be still, withdraw, know your truth.' And so, we work with this wisdom, we draw in upon ourselves, and look to the soft light of the Moon at this time for strength and inspiration.

SEPTEMBER

FULL MOON NAME

HARVEST MOON

The vibrant light of this month's full moon allowed the farmers and gatherers of the fields to harvest their crops late into the evening. Closest to the autumn equinox, this moon is a powerhouse of potential. Its extraordinary brightness hints at the joy of things to come. The perfect moment to give thanks for nature's abundance, this was a time of accomplishment and reward, but also a moment to plan, to wipe the slate clean of all that had gone before and to start afresh.

Adopt an attitude of gratitude this month. Give thanks for all the good things in your life and acknowledge your blessings every day.

MONTHLY FULL MOON RITUAL

Tap into your innate wisdom and create a 'moon stone' oracle with this ritual.

You will need: handful of stones of a similar size and hue, permanent marker pen, charm bag to keep them in

· To start, think of symbols that you can use to decorate your stones. For example, you might have a 'star' to represent success, a 'coin' to represent financial abundance, a 'heart' for love and a 'sun' for happiness. It's entirely up to you what symbols you choose and what they represent.

· To help, spend some time quietly gazing at the Moon for inspiration.

· Once you're happy with your selection, begin marking up your stones with the symbols, then add them to your bag.

· Close your eyes and ask the Moon to bless you with an intuitive message, shake the bag and pull out a stone.

· Let the symbol and the light of the Moon resonate within you.

FOLKLORE AND SUPERSTITIONS

LUNAR ECLIPSE MYTHS

Just like the full moon, a lunar eclipse is also full of magical potential. Around the world, superstitions are rife as to the fortuitous and sometimes ominous nature of this phenomenon. The ancients saw it as a time of transition when energy shifts and important events were more likely to happen.

The Batammaliba people of Toga and Benin tell the story of an ongoing war between the Sun and the Moon. The battle ensues during a lunar eclipse. While the people on Earth are fearful, they do their best to encourage a truce between the planets and peace soon follows. For this reason, the lunar eclipse is thought to be the ideal time to mend relationships and promote harmony within the community. In India, some people avoid eating during an eclipse, believing they're more likely to suffer indigestion.

MONTHLY NEW MOON RITUAL

Boost your self-confidence with a ritual that puts your talents in the spotlight.

· To begin, take a few deep breaths to clear your mind.

· Turn to a blank page in your journal and draw a large circle to represent the Moon. The circle also represents you and your gifts.

· Think about all the things you enjoy and do well and write some words in the circle.

· Think about your strengths and write these in the circle, too.

· Now think about your talents, the skills you were born with and could develop. Be honest and mention all the qualities that make you special, things like 'kindness', 'patience' and 'being a good listener'.

· When you're done, read through the words in your moon circle and acknowledge that these are your super powers. Consider how you might develop your gifts and use them more every day.

SEPTEMBER LUNAR FOOD

LEMON

It may be bright yellow in colour, but the juicy lemon has long been associated with the Moon, most likely because of its watery content. Used in magic to purify, it can eliminate negative energy, rejuvenate body and mind, and also bring joy and clarification. It's a popular ingredient in spells to attract positive energy, and can be consumed in a potion or brew, added to bathwater, sprinkled around the boundaries of the home for protection, or burnt as an oil to cleanse the home.

SPELL FOR ATTRACTING POSITIVE ENERGY AND GOOD FORTUNE

You will need: lemon, knife, sieve, boiling water, bucket and mop

Cast this spell: at night when the Moon is waxing

· Cut the lemon in half and squeeze the juice through a sieve into a bucket. Mix with a litre of boiling water.

· Swirl the mixture with a mop, then clean your floor as you would normally.

· As you do this, visualize a stream of lunar energy sweeping through your home and bathing the floor in golden light.

MOON DEITY

CERRIDWEN

Known as 'The Keeper of the Cauldron', this powerful Celtic goddess is associated with magic, creativity, wisdom and rebirth. An adept spell-caster, Cerridwen is famous for creating a potion to make her ugly son beautiful and wise. Knowing the elixir would take a year and a day to brew, she left her assistant Gwion in charge, but the young boy was careless and spilt drops upon his hand, which he quickly licked away. Infused with the power of the spell, he transformed into a rabbit. Cerridwen pursued him as a greyhound. The chase continued with both shape-shifting into different creatures until eventually Gwion changed into a grain of corn. Cerridwen, as a hen, ate him. Gwion was then reborn as Taliesin, the Welsh bard.

SPELL FOR THE CAULDRON OF ILLUMINATION

Boost your intuition by creating your own magical elixir.

You will need: saucepan, bundle of fresh rosemary, boiling water, spoon, sieve, cup, honey

· Place the rosemary (associated with personal power and the Moon) into the saucepan (to represent Cerridwen's cauldron) and cover with boiling water. Bring the mixture to the boil, then simmer for 10 minutes. Gently stir clockwise, while asking for a magical blessing.

· Strain the liquid through a sieve into a cup, then add a spoonful of honey. Relax and sip slowly.

· Pay attention to your thoughts over the next couple of days, as they may provide you with answers and insights.

CERRIDWEN

MOON SIGN OF THE MONTH

VIRGO

The lunar Virgo likes to get on with things. Analytical and down to earth, they take things step by step, and love being immersed in the finer details. It's no surprise that this sign is so organized, thanks to the orderly influence of Virgo. Nothing is too much trouble for others and these characters like to feel needed and useful in their circle of family and friends. Shy and retiring, this sign doesn't feel comfortable with big displays of emotion, instead they prefer to show they care by doing something practical. Routine is important: throw in a curveball and you'll see the lunar Virgo squirm. That said, they're extremely reliable, and always there in a crisis with no-nonsense advice and support.

MOON SPELL TO EMBRACE CHANGE AND GO WITH THE FLOW

You will need: jar with a lid, water, silver coin, pinch of salt

Cast this spell: during the waxing gibbous moon

· Fill the jar three-quarters full of water.

· Spend a couple of minutes breathing deeply to quieten your mind. The jar represents a wishing well and helps you connect with the watery element of the Moon's power.

· Take the silver coin in both hands, close your eyes and say:
'I cast this coin into the well, that it may seal this magic spell.
Of hands, of heart, of soul and mind, I embrace the future, as I find.'

· Drop the coin into the jar, followed by a pinch of salt for protection, then seal with the lid.

· Shake the jar gently and watch how the coin twists and turns in the water. Remember that life is fluid and that it is better to go with the flow than to resist it.

· Place the jar on a window sill in the light of the Moon.

OCTOBER

FULL MOON NAME

HUNTER'S MOON

The burnished glow of this month's full moon also gives it the title Blood Moon and Sanguine Moon, but it most commonly refers to the hunting season. The fields, now clear of crops, were open spaces where prey could be seen and predated with ease, and so it became the Hunter's Moon – a gift to those early tribes who needed to prepare for the long winter ahead. A herald to the change in seasons, this Moon's energy promotes transformation. Along with the chill in the air, there is a seismic shift in all things.

Relax into this lunar month, go with the flow and embrace the changes ahead.

MONTHLY FULL MOON RITUAL

Honour your ancestors and lost loved ones with a ritual that promotes love and healing.

You will need: table and tablecloth, photographs of passed loved ones, white flowers, vase, white candle, matches

· Imagine you're setting the table for a family gathering. You're going to honour lost loved ones by setting a place for them.

· Arrange the tablecloth and position the photographs around the table to represent those who have passed on.

· Place the white flowers in a vase in the centre of the table.

· Light the candle and take a seat at the table.

· Close your eyes and open your heart.

· Think about all the people you have invited and what they mean to you. Bring to mind any cherished memories and give thanks for each person.

· Feel the love that surrounds you at this moment and draw it in with each breath.

· Use this time to reflect upon where you are in life, and the wonderful people who have accompanied you on your journey.

FOLKLORE AND SUPERSTITIONS

MOON MADNESS AND MYTHS

The ancients believed that the Moon was at the height of its powers when it was full and that this could affect the conduct of humans and animals. This erratic energy spawned the word 'lunacy', which evolved from the Latin *luna* meaning 'moon'. It was thought that the pull of the Moon upon the tides of the Earth sparked strange behaviour.

The Ancient Greeks noted the howling of wolves during a full moon, and so the myth of the werewolf was born. To them, it seemed feasible that a man could transform into a wolf and display feral tendencies during this lunar phase, and folk tales supported this theory. One particular myth cites the plight of Lycaon, a mortal man who was transformed into a wolf by the gods as punishment for attempting to trick Zeus into eating human flesh.

MONTHLY NEW MOON RITUAL

Clear your mind of clutter with a soothing meditation.

You will need: amethyst healing point, cushion

· Lay down and rest your head on a cushion. Place an amethyst point over the centre of your forehead, where your third-eye energy centre is located. This energy centre helps to activate your intuition.

· Close your eyes and take a long deep breath in. Imagine that your breath travels like a stream of white light through the top of your head, along your neck and into your chest and stomach. As you release the breath, it travels along each leg and out through the soles of your feet.

· Continue breathing in this way, bringing the light in through your head and out through your feet.

· Imagine that each breath is filled with lunar light sweeping through your body, clearing away negative energy.

· After a couple of minutes, turn your attention to the centre of your forehead. Imagine a window of light opening up, allowing the lunar energy to flow freely.

· Let your mind expand and absorb the light. Breathe and relax.

OCTOBER LUNAR FOOD

RICE

White rice is considered a lunar food, mostly because of its colour, which corresponds with the Moon's lunar light. A popular choice at Chinese New Year, it's thought to be extremely lucky and is eaten to promote good fortune. While it's linked to the Moon, it is also associated with the earth element, and used in spells for abundance and protection. A popular folk magic practice involved leaving a bowl of rice by the door to distract evil spirits. It was thought that the harmful entities would spend their time counting each grain, which delayed them from entering the home.

SPELL FOR ATTRACTING GOOD FORTUNE

You will need: small clean jar with a lid, cup of uncooked white rice, silver coin, pen and paper

Cast this spell: at any phase during the lunar cycle

- Fill the jar with the rice and add in the silver coin, which represents success and prosperity.

- Write your wish for good fortune on the paper. Keep it simple, something like:
  'May good luck bless me and my home.'

- Screw the paper into a ball and pop it in the jar.

- Place the jar by your front door, so that every time you enter and leave you can give it a shake and then repeat your wish out loud, or in your head.

- Continue to do this for one lunar cycle to reap the benefits.

MOON DEITY

SIN

Also known as Nanna, Sin was a Mesopotamian god of the Moon. Mostly associated with the crescent moon, he was revered for the power of prosperity and his ability to affect fertility, particularly that of the cow herds of the people who lived near the marshes of the lower Euphrates river. Sin governed the rise and flow of the water, the growth of the reeds and also the health of the herds, and was often depicted with bull horns on his head. His heavenly consort was the beautiful goddess of the reeds, Ningal, and his son was Shamash, the vibrant god of the Sun. To his people, Sin was a key deity, and essential for their survival. He would appear as an old, fatherly man, with a trailing beard and a crown of four horns upon his head.

SPELL FOR THE WISHING SYMBOL

Make a magical wish inspired by Sin's association with all things dairy.

You will need: piece of cheese (or cheese substitute), pin or knife

· To begin, think about your wish and what it represents. Decide on a symbol that represents your wish, for example a coin for wealth or a heart for love.

· Carve the symbol into a small square of cheese. Say: *'I wish for this, I make it mine, from this moment forwards to the end of time.'*

· Either eat the cheese or take it outside and crumble into tiny pieces as an offering to the birds.

SIN

MOON SIGN OF THE MONTH

LIBRA

Lunar Librans like to appear balanced and will do everything in their power to keep the status quo, but deep down there's a need to fix things. Perfection is their aim, particularly in relationships, and partnerships are especially key. This moon sign loves to be loved, and only feels secure in a nurturing relationship. Friendship, too, is important, and they will always seek company rather than being alone. Harmony is what drives them, but their idealistic view of life can lead to discontent as they strive for something that is not continually attainable. Lunar Librans do have a lighter side and are extremely charming and flirtatious, which makes them a joy to be around.

MOON SPELL TO GIVE YOURSELF A LOVING BOOST

You will need: handful of white tealights, rose quartz, white rose petals, matches

Cast this spell: during the waning phase of the Moon

· Start by arranging the tealights into a crescent shape to represent the gentle power of the waning moon. This lunar phase will help you nourish your heart and soul with loving energy.

· Place the rose quartz in the centre of the arc. This generous stone is associated with self-esteem and can help you be kind to yourself.

· Sprinkle the petals around the stone to represent your natural beauty.

· Light each of the tealights and spend a few minutes looking at the display you have created. Say:
'I am enough, for I am me. I love myself, my heart is free.'

· Let the candles burn down, then remove the rose quartz and keep it with you as a charm for self-love.

NOVEMBER

FULL MOON NAME

BEAVER MOON

As the blanket of winter settles at our feet, the animal kingdom follows suit, preparing for the coming freeze. The beavers, who are mainly nocturnal, work beneath the light of this full moon to build their dams. They sense the shift in seasons and the need to go within, and so this month's lunar title pays homage to their cause. Also known as the Frost Moon, to mark the drop in temperature, and the Trading Moon.

This full moon urges you to take your lead from the creatures of the land. Make the time to recharge and nurture your body, mind and soul.

MONTHLY FULL MOON RITUAL

Recharge this full moon with a breathing exercise to calm and brighten your mood.

· Close your eyes and imagine you are sitting high upon a mountain beneath the light of the full moon. As you look down, you can see the valley unfolding before you. The contrast of light and dark, as the shadows gather, creates a sense of peace and balance.

· You breathe in the beauty of the moonlit landscape.

· As you inhale, count to the beat of four, and as you exhale, lengthen the count to five, cleansing your body and mind of any negative energy.

· Take your time with each breath and draw in the stillness.
  Feel it settle in the centre of your chest and hold it there.

· As you exhale, release any fear or anxiety.

FOLKLORE AND SUPERSTITIONS

SIBERIAN MOON MYTHS

The Ket tribe of Siberia have a powerful myth about the
creation of the crescent moon. A brother and sister live
in heart of the forest. The brother catches the eye of the
Sun Maiden, and she carries him off into the sky using her
vibrant rays. While he is happy being her consort, he misses
home and begs to visit. In his absence, his sister has been
devoured by a horrible witch, who tries to kill the brother
on his return.

The brother flees on horseback, but the witch grasps at
his skin with her claw-like fingers. The Sun Maiden tries
desperately to pull him free, but in the tussle the brother
is torn in two. The Sun does her best to revive him, but the
half she holds is missing a heart, and so he dies, over and
over again. In the end, he is banished to the other side of the
heavens, as the crescent moon. It is only on the longest day
of the year that the Sun and the Moon are reunited.

MONTHLY NEW MOON RITUAL

Give self-esteem a boost with the help of the new moon.

· Set the evening aside for you. Imagine you are on a special date. How would you like to feel?

· Create the perfect setting, with beautiful white blooms to represent the Moon, and scented candles. Scatter petals in circular and crescent patterns at your feet to represent the Moon's phases.

· Sit and be happy in your own company.

· Think about all the wonderful qualities and traits that make you unique. Write a love letter to yourself outlining these things.

· Finish the note by saying:
'*I love you! You are wonderful.*'

· Enjoy spending time with yourself and acknowledge that you are beautiful.

LETTUCE

Luscious and leafy, the lettuce is a lunar food because of its light and often translucent appearance, along with its watery content – a nod to the Moon's influence upon the tides. Easy to grow, it was a popular food choice of the ancients, who would sow and transplant plants during the new moon phase. They believed that the Moon had an impact on its growth, and that the best time to plant lettuce was when the Moon was waxing. Used in magic for healing, protection and peace, lettuce is renowned for its sleep-inducing properties.

SPELL FOR A RIFT IN ANY RELATIONSHIP

You will need: 5 large lettuce leaves, saucepan, boiling water, sieve, 2 cups, sprig of mint, pinch of ground nutmeg

· Place the lettuce leaves in a saucepan and cover with boiling water. Simmer for about 10 minutes.

· Strain the water into two cups and add the mint leaves to promote love and healing. Add a pinch of ground nutmeg for protection.

· Share this magical brew with the person that you'd like to reach out to.

· As you drink, ask for the healing energy to flow between you and heal any rifts.

MOON DEITY

LUNA

This pale-skinned Roman goddess, with flowing dark hair, was often depicted riding her spectral chariot through the night sky. Sometimes pulled by a yoke of oxen and sometimes a pair of silvery scaled dragons, Luna was the epitome of enchantment, particularly on a full moon. Patron of all things feminine, Luna governed childbirth, fertility and love, and offered protection to charioteers.

It was thought that Luna gave birth to a new moon each month, making her a powerful mother goddess and part of a triad of deities, which included Hecate, goddess of the underworld, and Diana, goddess of the Earth. Associated with the owl and the raven, Luna was often called upon for her second sight and intuition.

SPELL FOR THE FEATHER OF FORTUNE

Make a charm to connect with Luna's uplifting energy and attract good luck.

You will need: large white feather, white thread or ribbon

- Place the feather on a window ledge beneath the light of the full moon and leave overnight.

- In the morning, take the thread and wrap it around the stem of the feather three times to represent the heavenly triad, of which Luna was a part.

- Secure the thread to the feather with a knot, then hang it somewhere near your front door to draw positive energy into your home.

LUNA

MOON SIGN OF THE MONTH

SCORPIO

There's an emotional intensity to lunar Scorpios that can be both intoxicating and intimidating. Those who enter into a relationship with this sign must be prepared for a mix of passion and drama. Life is far from boring and should it ever feel that way, they will do their very best to shake things up. While most people tend to avoid trials and tribulations, this sign thrives upon a challenge, particularly one that involves mastering the emotions. Being both intelligent and perceptive, they're able to read people and situations and have a knack for simply 'knowing' the truth. At times, it can seem like they see into the heart and soul of a person, which makes them even more intriguing to be around.

MOON SPELL TO EMPTY THE MIND OF WORRY AND STRESS

You will need: bowl, warm water, lavender and rosemary essential oils, dark flannel

Cast this spell: any time during the waxing crescent moon

· Half-fill a small bowl with warm water. Add 7 drops of lavender essential oil and 3 drops of rosemary. Lavender promotes peaceful energy and rosemary is a powerful cleanser.

· Place the flannel in the bowl and leave for a couple of minutes, then retrieve and squeeze to remove excess water.

· Lie down and fold the flannel over your forehead.

· Picture a room behind your eyes, a space that houses all your thoughts. As you inhale, you take in all that calm energy and it sweeps through this space like a gentle wind.

· As you exhale, release any worry or stress in your outward breath. Say:
'Peace is mine from this moment in time. As I breathe, this gift I receive.'

WINTER

The stark cry of winter calls to something deep inside. Ethereal and naked, we may shiver in its wake, but it is not without mercy. This is the season of love, when all around goes to ground. The cooling of the earth brings clarity and a renewed sense of wonder, just as the dark of the Moon provides a comfort blanket to the soul. This is the time to ponder, to delight and wander the corridors of imagination, to release the past and the withered leaves of regret that bind you and say, 'I am here, this is the essence of me.' When we embrace the power of the season and the dark of the Moon, we have traversed the cycle, we have learnt to go with the flow, and we are ready to accept our true nature.

DECEMBER

COLD MOON

As the biting chill gnaws at the landscape, the Cold Moon casts its ghostly glow. Named after the harsh weather that clings to its lunar rays, it is also known as the Moon before Yule, as it heralds the winter solstice, and the Long Night's Moon. Holding court in the heavens for all to see, its ethereal light seeps beneath the skin with spectral fingers, searching for what truly matters.

It is time to acknowledge any pain and release it. Clear a path for the future and trust that you have all the answers you need.

MONTHLY FULL MOON RITUAL

Create a memory box, to boost positive energy.

You will need: decorative box, lots of coloured paper, pen, photographs, other meaningful mementos

· To begin, think about how to make the box special. You might want to line it with coloured tissue paper, cover it in jewels, beads and glitter, or decorate it in some other way.

· Make a list of special memories and write a few words about each one on different pieces of paper. Add photographs that remind you of happy times and any other mementos.

· Add meaningful quotes and poems that help you recall significant moments from your past.

· Once you've filled the box, make a point of dipping into it at least once a week to pull out a memory. Relive the experience and enjoy all the joyful emotions associated with it.

· Add new memories to your box as they happen, to keep the positive energy alive.

FOLKLORE AND SUPERSTITIONS

MOON-EATING MONSTERS

In the Bicol region of the Philippines, stories of a moon-eating monster called the Bakunawa are told. This enormous serpent-like creature emerges from the sea to gobble up the Moon. Originally a stunning goddess who fell in love with the moon god Bulan, she tried everything to win his favour, from lighting up the sky with stars, to sending the sweetest birds to sing for him. Unfortunately, Bulan did not return her love. In her anger, she transformed into a scaly serpent and tried to devour both Bulan and his sister Haliya, the goddess of moonlight, but could not defeat them. The Supreme God was enraged by her behaviour and cursed her to remain in this demonic form as punishment. She continues to plague Bulan and Haliya, but they stay safe by hiding parts of themselves each month.

MONTHLY NEW MOON RITUAL

Visualize the future with a ritual to open your heart and mind.

You will need: cushions and blankets, a space to sit – preferably in view of the night sky

- Arrange the cushions and blankets so that you have somewhere comfortable to sit. Think of this as a safe space where you can relax and ponder the future.

- Gaze at the night sky, at the vast expanse of darkness and the infinite possibilities it holds. Inhale and feel the stillness.

- Close your eyes and picture the future. To start, you might picture an event in the immediate future, or take yourself a month, or six months, forward.

- Imagine you're watching a film of what will happen. See yourself achieving your goals and standing in the light and in your power. Engage your emotions and all your senses to make this as real as possible.

- When you're ready, open your eyes and give your body a shake. Know that your thoughts have the power to manifest your dreams.

DECEMBER LUNAR FOOD

CLOVES

Traditionally, cloves are linked to the element of fire and the planet Jupiter, but they also have an association with the Moon, and are often used in rituals and spells around the time of the new moon. Historically, they were burnt to rid the home from harmful energy, used in pomanders, and crumbled to dust and scattered along boundaries and underfoot to offer protection, and to prevent gossip. Their warm fragrant scent is often associated with the festive season.

SPELL FOR PROMOTING FRIENDSHIP AND HARMONY

You will need: large orange, peeler, decorative bowl, 3–4 pinecones, handful of cloves

Cast this spell: best performed during a new moon

· Remove some of the orange peel and separate the orange into segments.

· Arrange the orange segments in the bowl with the pine cones. Oranges are associated with happiness, while pinecones represent good fortune.

· Scatter the cloves over the top. As you do so, make a wish that friendship will flourish and joy will spread under the beneficial rays of the new moon.

· Scatter the orange peel over the top of your arrangement.

· Position the bowl in the centre of a table at mealtimes, or when you have a gathering of friends and family, to promote harmony and the flow of conversation.

HECATE

Known as the Queen of the Witches and the Goddess of Crossroads, the mighty Hecate juggled many responsibilities. Associated with magic and prophecy, she walked the dark places, from the underworld to the dead of night, bringing illumination with her lunar light. A triple goddess, she embraced the three aspects of womanhood: Maiden, Mother and Crone, favouring the latter guise most, for this was where she could draw upon her innate wisdom. Usually accompanied by a pack of dogs and carrying a torch, it was thought that if you stood at the centre of a crossroads during the dark of the moon, you would see a vision of this goddess.

SPELL FOR THE CROSSROAD CANDLE MAGIC

Use the help of Hecate's crossroads to come to a decision between two paths.

You will need: piece of paper, pen, black candle, matches

· Draw a large cross on a piece of paper. Along the horizontal line, write one course of action; on the vertical, write the other. Place the candle in the centre and light it.

· Close your eyes and ask Hecate to help you tune into your inner wisdom. Say:
'*I have all the answers I seek today; may the light fall to reveal the way.*'

· Open your eyes and look at the flame. How does it lean? Does it favour one direction more than the other?

· Spend a few moments focusing on the flame. Look to your thoughts for signs to help you move forwards.

HECATE

SAGITTARIUS

Lunar Sagittarians are gregarious and open-minded. There's nothing they love more than to explore, learning about different cultures and ways of being. They enjoy imparting their knowledge, too. Their innate belief that all will work out for the best means they rarely plan and prefer to seize the day. Freedom-loving and spirited, they cannot be hemmed in, and tend to avoid serious commitment unless it allows some wiggle room. That said, they do enjoy being with others, but emotional dramas make them run for the hills. Travel is high on their list of necessities, and they're never in one place for long, which makes for some interesting stories!

MOON SPELL TO STEP OUTSIDE YOUR COMFORT ZONE

You will need: paper, pen, sprigs of rosemary, fireproof bowl, black pepper, lighter or matches

Cast this spell: during the build-up to a full moon

· Imagine you could do anything or go anywhere in the world. What would you like to do? Even if your dreams seem unreachable, bring them to mind and imagine what it would be like to make them real.

· Think of a word to sum up the experience. For example, 'excitement' or 'fun'. Write this on a small piece of paper.

· Add a few sprigs of rosemary to the bowl. This herb represents personal power and is associated with the Moon's energy.

· Throw in a pinch of black pepper for protection.

· Take the lighter or a match and pass the paper through the flame, then drop it into the bowl and let it burn. Say: *'As I wish, as I hope, as I see. May I bring my dream to me.'*

MOON CALENDARS

2024 LUNAR PHASES

New Moon ○	First Quarter ◗	Full Moon ●	Third Quater ◗
January 11	January 18	January 25	January 4
February 9	February 16	February 24	February 2
March 10	March 17	March 25	March 3
April 8	April 15	April 24	April 2
May 8	May 15	May 23	May 1, 30
June 6	June 14	June 22	June 28
July 5	July 13	July 21	July 28
August 4	August 12	August 19	August 26
September 3	September 11	September 18	September 24
October 2	October 10	October 17	October 24
November 1	November 9	November 15	November 23
December 1, 30	December 8	December 15	December 22

2025 LUNAR PHASES

New Moon ○	First Quarter ◗	Full Moon ●	Third Quater ◗
January 29	January 6	January 13	January 21
Feb. 28	Feb. 5	Feb. 12	Feb. 20
March 29	March 6	March 14	March 22
April 27	April 5	April 13	April 21
May 27	May 4	May 12	May 20
June 25	June 3	June 11	June 18
July 24	July 2	July 10	July 18
August 23	August 1, 31	August 9	August 16
September 21	September 30	September 7	September 14
October 21	October 29	October 7	October 23
November 20	November 28	November 5	November 12
December 20	December 27	December 4	December 11

2026 LUNAR PHASES

New Moon ○	First Quarter ◗	Full Moon ●	Third Quater ◗
January 26	January 5	January 12	January 18
February 25	February 3	February 10	February 17
March 26	March 4	March 11	March 17
April 24	April 2	April 9	April 16
May 24	May 2, 31	May 8	May 16
June 22	June 29	June 7	June 15
July 22	July 28	July 6	July 14
August 20	August 27	August 5	August 13
September 18	September 25	September 4	September 12
October 18	October 25	October 3	October 11
November 16	November 24	November 2	November 9
December 16	December 23	December 2, 31	December 9

2027 LUNAR PHASES

New Moon ○	First Quarter ◗	Full Moon ●	Third Quater ◖
January 18	January 26	January 3	January 10
Feb. 17	Feb. 24	Feb. 1	Feb. 9
March 19	March 25	March 3	March 11
April 17	April 24	April 2	April 10
May 16	May 23	May 1, 31	May 9
June 15	June 21	June 30	June 8
July 14	July 21	July 29	July 7
August 12	August 20	August 28	August 6
September 11	September 18	September 26	September 4
October 10	October 18	October 26	October 3
November 9	November 17	November 24	November 1
December 9	December 17	December 24	December 1, 30

2028 LUNAR PHASES

New Moon ○	First Quarter ◗	Full Moon ●	Third Quater ◖
January 7	January 15	January 22	January 29
Feb. 6	Feb. 14	Feb. 20	Feb. 28
March 8	March 15	March 22	March 30
April 7	April 13	April 20	April 28
May 6	May 13	May 20	May 28
June 4	June 11	June 19	June 27
July 4	July 10	July 18	July 26
August 2, 31	August 9	August 17	August 25
September 30	September 7	September 16	September 23
October 29	October 7	October 15	October 22
November 28	November 6	November 14	November 21
December 27	December 6	December 13	December 20

2029 LUNAR PHASES

New Moon ○	First Quarter ◗	Full Moon ●	Third Quater ◖
January 14	January 22	January 30	January 7
February 13	February 21	February 28	February 5
March 15	March 23	March 30	March 7
April 13	April 21	April 28	April 5
May 13	May 21	May 27	May 5
June 12	June 19	June 26	June 4
July 11	July 18	July 25	July 3
August 10	August 16	August 24	August 2
September 8	September 15	September 22	September 1, 30
October 7	October 14	October 22	October 30
November 6	November 13	November 21	November 28
December 5	December 12	December 20	December 28

ABOUT THE AUTHOR

A professional storyteller with a keen interest in mythology, spirituality and the natural world, Alison Davies is the author of over thirty books, including *The Mystical Year* and *The Self-Care Year*. She also runs writing workshops at universities across the United Kingdom.

ACKNOWLEDGEMENTS

I would like to thank my brilliant editor Sofie, for helping me shape this book and make it into something truly special. I would also like to thank the amazing Anastasia for her stunning artwork and cover, and Katy the designer, for having such a wonderful eye and making everything stand out on the page. The magic of these three, and the rest of the team at Quadrille, has made this book shine like the glistening orb it celebrates.

MANAGING DIRECTOR
Sarah Lavelle

ASSISTANT EDITOR
Sofie Shearman

DESIGNER
Katy Everett

ILLUSTRATOR
Anastasia Stefurak

HEAD OF PRODUCTION
Stephen Lang

PRODUCTION CONTROLLER
Martina Georgieva

Published in 2023 by Quadrille,
an imprint of Hardie Grant Publishing

Quadrille
52–54 Southwark Street
London SE1 1UN
quadrille.com

Cataloguing in Publication Data: a catalogue record for this book
is available from the British Library.

ISBN 978 1 83783 090 9

Printed in China

MIX
Paper | Supporting
responsible forestry
FSC™ C020056